STARTERS
PEOPLE

The Wright Brothers

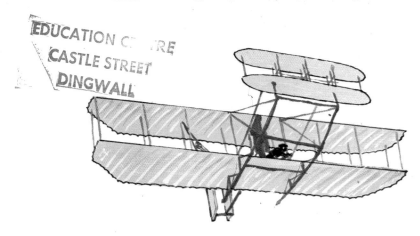

Macdonald Educational

This is a jet aeroplane.
It flies very fast.
It can carry hundreds of people.

Long ago there were no aeroplanes.
These are some of the first aeroplanes.
They did not fly properly.

3

Wilbur and Orville Wright lived in America.
They were interested in things that flew.
Their father gave them a toy helicopter.
It could fly.

4

The Wright brothers wanted to find out
how things flew.
They played with paper darts.
They made kites.
They watched birds flying.

When they were older,
the brothers opened a bicycle shop.
They mended bicycles.

6

Then they made their own bicycle.
It was called the Van Cleeve bicycle.

Otto Lilienthal's
glider

The brothers read about this German glider.
Gliders do not have engines.
The Wright brothers wanted to make
their own gliders.

8

This was their first glider.
They flew it like a kite.

frame

plans

Then they made much bigger gliders.
A man could fly in them.
First they made a frame of wood.
10

They covered the frame with cloth.
Their sister sewed the cloth for them.

They flew the glider near a place
called Kitty Hawk.
Kitty Hawk was bare and windy.
It was a good place to fly a glider.
12

Soon their glider flew very well.
The two brothers took it in turn
to fly it.

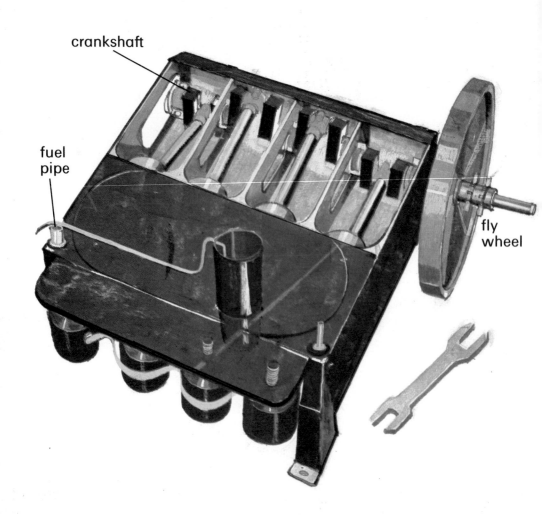

crankshaft

fuel
pipe

fly
wheel

Next the brothers made an aeroplane.
It had an engine.
They built their own engine.

14

They built their own propellers.
The propellers were made of wood.

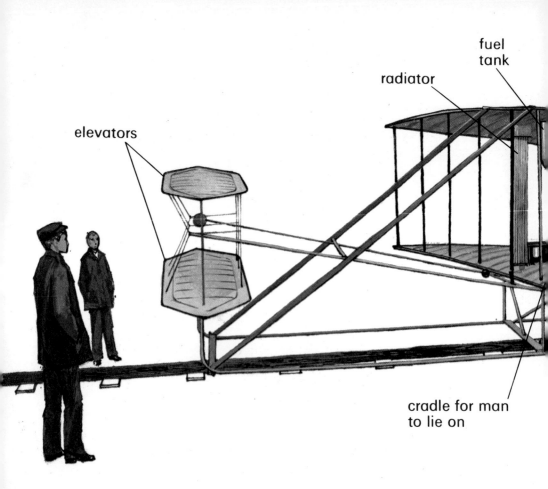

elevators

radiator

fuel tank

cradle for man to lie on

When they had finished all the parts,
the aeroplane looked like this.
The aeroplane had two wings.

16

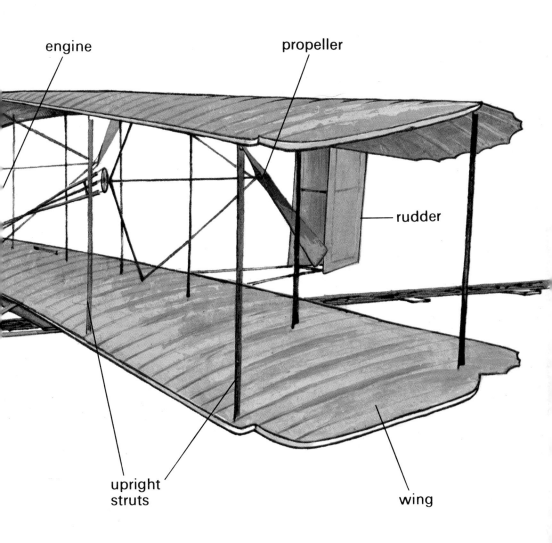

engine

propeller

rudder

upright
struts

wing

Now Wilbur and Orville were ready
to try out their new aeroplane.

17

The aeroplane flew through the air.
It stayed in the air for almost a minute.
This aeroplane was the first in the world
to fly properly.

18

They soon made a better aeroplane.
It could turn and make circles
in the air.

Wilbur took a new aeroplane to France.
He wanted to show people
how well it could fly.

He took the aeroplane to a large open space.
Thousands of people came to watch him fly.

Orville stayed in America.
One day he took a passenger on a flight.
The aeroplane crashed.
The passenger was killed.

The Wright brothers opened a big workshop.
They made many aeroplanes there.

Other people copied the ideas
of the Wright brothers.
Voisin made this aeroplane.
24

A man called Blériot flew this aeroplane
over the English Channel.
It was the first aeroplane
to fly over the sea.

25

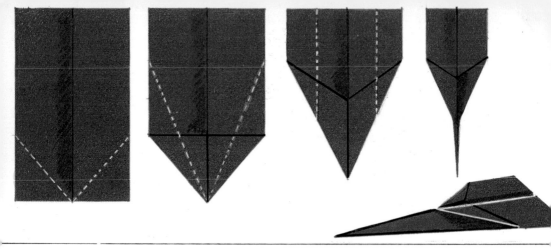

Can you make a glider like this?
Paint your own pattern on the wings.
26

Index

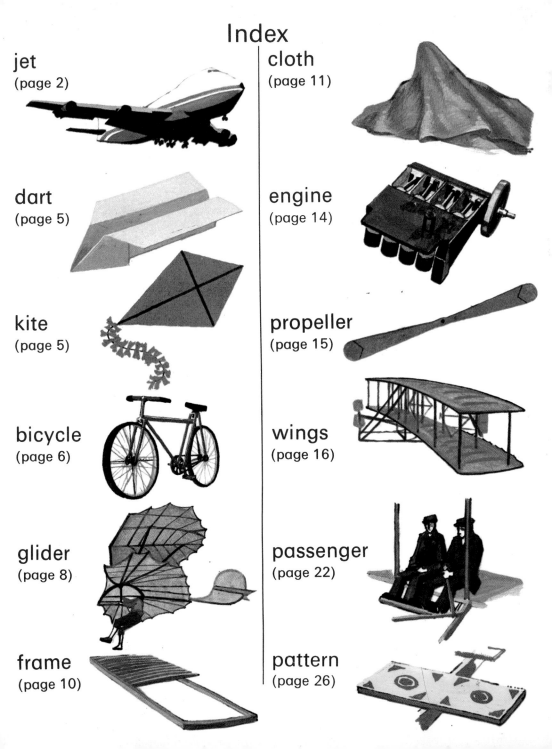

The story of flight

People have always wanted to fly. At first men tried
to fly with wings strapped to their arms.
But their muscles were not strong enough
to keep them in the air for very long.

Then men flew in balloons. The balloons were filled
with hot air. Next men filled balloons with gas.
Gas balloons travelled further than hot air balloons.
Other balloons were driven by engines.
They were called airships.

Then men learned to make gliders. Gliders have
fixed wings. The wings of gliders float in the air
like kites. Gliders do not have engines.

The Wright brothers built an aeroplane with an
engine. It was the first aeroplane to fly properly.
After the Wright brothers people made many
different kinds of aeroplanes. Some of them carry
only one man, others can carry hundreds of people.